The Creator's Touch

The Creator's Touch

Poems

CAMELLIA SMITH STADTS

2024

GOLDEN DRAGONFLY PRESS

AMHERST, MASSACHUSETTS

FIRST PRINT EDITION, June 2024
FIRST EBOOK EDITION, July 2024

ISBN: 979–8–9894116–2–7

Library of Congress Control Number: Requested

Printed on acid-free paper supplied by a Forest Stewardship Council-certified
provider. First published in the United States of America by Golden Dragonfly
Press, 2024.

www.goldendragonflypress.com

I am dedicating this book of poetry
to my son Nick,
my daughter Carolyn,
and my grandson Cameren.

Contents

For the Bees

Look under petals.
Around the block
down concrete highways
through Mall parking lots

Where have we gone?
Left without a trace.
We could no longer keep up.
Your demanding pace.

You take us places,
we do not even know,
and expect us to call
wherever you dump us, home.

The pesticides used.
You could not understand.
Goucho, Poncho,
they need to be banned.

The sugar water you feed us
will not keep us strong.
More poison you give us
all winter long.

So where have we gone?
You ask, scratching your heads.
We are in the Divine Mothers arms
where we are safe from all harm.

You will not think to look there.
You are no longer wise.
Your arrogance has blinded you
to your own demise.

Mirrors

The day I look in the mirror
and see only someone
who is weary, tired, old.

How did this person get here?
I close my eyes, open them.
And look again hoping to see
the happy, somewhat pretty girl
that laughed a lot. But was she real?

Or was she fabricated
by the alcohol consumed
or the makeup she wore?

Did she know herself then?
Does she know herself now?

Can she trust herself
to love herself regardless of what
she sees in the mirror—

What she has been told her whole life
from those who were supposed
to be on her side, lift her up,
believe in her but never did.
Or at least never showed it.

It always came as a shock to know
that if there was anything good in her,
she would have to hear it from herself.

And so It Goes...

I cannot stop.
I cannot doubt.
The words that flow
from my heart to yours

The world keeps turning,
too fast at times.
I grasp and cling
to slow it down

And if I feel
I have succeeded,
then what?
The words that were once

So clear, so desperate
to be spoken
vanish like smoke
before my eyes

Only to turn up
in another form,
similar, yet different,
and so it goes…

A Trusting Heart

Can you make it tomorrow?

Can you make it today?

Take just one step.

One small step into the future.

You don't even have to know

where you are going.

You can have your eyes open or closed.

The Spirit leads, so eyes are not necessary.

Only a willing heart, a brave heart.

A beautiful, strong trusting heart.

Ode to Desire

Fan stirs the air,
lifting the sheet
like a determined lover

Caressing my thigh.
I lie still,
grateful for its touch

Giving my skin
familiar stirrings
I usually get from hot hands.

Release me from the heat
with your cool embrace.

Dreams and Other Fairy Tales

Sinking deep as the moon makes its descent from the sky.
I'm falling into dreams that have me sharing my night
with the stars.
I reach for a comet that flies overhead, but remains nowhere close,
except in my dreams.
My dreams surround me with colors of coral and turquoise.
I realize that I have fallen to the ocean depths,
trusting my dreams to not let me drown.
I slowly rise to the surface of my journey to the underworld
that leaves me wet and wondering as I float to the top of
my consciousness.
How did I manage to fall so easily?

Awaiting Spring

Deep calls to deep,
a love hidden.
April in Michigan,
every day looking
out my window
seven floors below
where a barren
garden awaits,
warmth from the sun
encouraging eager
hands to dig deep,
and plant
a hopeful harvest
come Fall.

Ode to Metamorphosis

Silver Age brings co-creation.
Demeter blesses the sweat of man's brow.
Corn, barley and grapes bring bread and wine
to restore man's strength for another day.

Recognize where the gift comes from.
Your work, o'man is in vain if not blessed.
Prayers, incense rise up to the mysteries.
Demeter's gift of fertile soil, Gaia cradles the seed.

Apollo gives warmth from the sun, Zeus gives showers.
Even the bee cannot give honey unless the flower grows.
The bee must work for its own nourishment and ours.
Slaves to the gods you mortals must be throughout your days.

Seasons change, time is fleeting and too soon the cold wind blows.
Ice covers the once pregnant soil which held an abundance of life.
The cold will not last. In due season Persephone will return
bringing fertility with her, by her mother's grace.

The Creator's Touch

The first flash of lightning
followed by the loud crack of thunder
wakes me to the present moment.
The daydream that had me so wrapped
in its grip eludes me now.
How easy to forget when nature steps in
to remind us what is really important,
the here and now,
what's right in front of us.
What is most vital and yet,
sadly, so easy to ignore.
Giving thanks to my Creator and the Creator of all
for the touches to my senses that bring me back
to where I need to be.

Sometimes

Why do sometimes,
the words fade,
and sometimes flow?

They can be as pretty as flowers,
or course as grit
between teeth on a windy day

Sometimes you can pick
and choose and sometimes
you have no choice

But to just write it all down
and hope to know, someday,
what it all means.

The Litany of a Small Life

My love flows toward the long forgotten Catholic rituals.
Growing up with evening Masses for special Feast days.
I cherish those memories of darkened pews
and the smell of candles and incense that felt
more prominent after the sun went down.
The statues of Mary and Jesus would glow
in the candlelight that made them seem to come alive.

During the Mass, a Litany would be chanted
by the almost full church.
Litanies, at those times, in Latin making it
even more mystical and sacred to my eight-year-old eyes and ears
Sancta Maria, ora pro nobis, te rogamus audi nos
Rosa Mystica, ora pro nobis, te rogamus audi nos

I would soon lose myself in an almost trance-like state
by the repetition and holiness of it all.
Afterwards, filing out through the wide church doors
out into the cold night air, stopping to look up.
At the clear star-filled sky and knew that
I had touched God this night.

Creativity

Creativity is a gift
that opens up
inside yourself
bursting with colors,
ideas, love, and joy

Sometimes it stays
for days.
Sometimes just hours,
moments, or seconds.
You always have
to be ready when it comes

Grab a pen, pencil, crayon,
paintbrush and just let it flow.
Block out the world
and trust what's inside, always.
Even if it's not million-dollar
material, it's still your gift
to the world

When God created the world
He let loose,
making some things weird,
ugly and downright questionable.
But other things made by God

Are stunning in their beauty
and uniqueness.
All were created good in God's eyes.
No matter what you create,
it is all good in God's eyes,
so it should be in your eyes as well.

Hope Floats

I think of those
in flood-ravaged areas,
the farmers,
those that lost every single
thing to water
that refused to stop falling.

The devastation that no one
can point fingers at,
maybe God. Some of
them do that. They need
a reason, someone to
get angry at.

Hopelessness, the sinking
feeling in their hearts,
as the mud and water
rise to new levels
with more on the way

Those in the middle of
it all know that things

are beyond the point
of saving anything,
although they still have
their lives and each other.

The sun when it finally
comes out again
to start over.

Woodpeckers

I love woodpeckers.
I do not see them,
but when Spring
is slowly beginning,
I hear them.

High up in the trees
as the bugs begin
to stir and the sap
starts to run,
they are ready.

They know
the perfect trees
to begin their knocking
and hammering
to drill through the bark.

I love the woodpeckers.
As with other signs of Spring
I recognize in them the beginning
of the turn of the seasons.

Healing My Heart

My heart is broken.
It has been for a long time.
The brokenness comes from
hiding my tears, believing the lies,
stuffing down feelings
with food day after day.
It feels safe.
I have always believed food
was one thing that would not
hurt me, but I was wrong.
For years my heart
has become damaged
by ignoring the warning signs
and continuing to do
what I have always done.
But I am learning, slowly learning,
that my ways had built
a false sense of security
and that love for myself
is more true and healing,
feeling the love as I slowly let go
of whatever I thought would save me
and be free…
Believing in myself is freedom,
freedom is love.
This love can heal my heart.

False Starts

The days continue
to be cold and dreary,
no life outside
except the birds,
always the birds,
and the squirrels,
silent but ever active.

A few warm days
earlier in the month
brought flowers
showing their faces
way too early in April.
They should have known better.
It happens every year.

We don't know any better
either, do we?
First hint of warmth
and we are putting
winter clothes in storage.
That is the hope that slowly,
slowly brings the sunshine.

Freedom

I have never been locked
in a jail cell, but I have
spent too much time
in cells of my own making.

The cell of insecurity
The cell of shame
The cell of anger
The cell of hate
The cell of pain,
to name just a few.

To turn the page and start over
like someone who has been
behind bars for so long
and is finally set free
whether there was guilt or innocence,
there has to be

A choice made to move forward.
Without looking back.
To believe in
your own worth
and to be brave enough to share the love
that has been buried far too deep
for far too long.

Hiccups and Earthquakes

Hiccups are the blips,
and burps of our life.
They are not painful,
so much as just a pain in the ass,
or hurtful, but not devastating.
I will not name any here.
Everybody's hiccups
are different or seen as different
by each person.
What some people see as hiccups,
others see as earthquakes.

Now earthquakes for most people
are something that hits us out of nowhere.
They knock us down hard
and leave us wondering
what happened.
Why did that happen or how
could that happen?

For some, every hiccup
can become an earthquake—
getting blindsided by something.
Anything can ruin a perfectly
good day—put you in a funk
that takes days
or even weeks to get over.
Those who find themselves
knocked down by what
they see as yet another earthquake,
find it harder and harder
to get up and move on.
They need help.

They need help from those of us
who have survived earthquakes
in our own lives and have been able
to pick ourselves back up
a little stronger and understanding
of ourselves and others.
We are the ones who need
to hold up those that cannot
seem to hold themselves up.
That is love, that is compassion.
How long, you may ask,
must we do this? As long as it takes.
There will always be another one.
Waiting to be saved from
an earthquake in their life—
you cannot let them go under,
or slip through the cracks.

That is your gift, that is your calling.

Blessings of Watercolor 1

My brush poised,
just above the paper
after being dipped
in water and paint

I make a slow,
mindful line of Crimson Red
right down the center
of the page.

I dip the brush once again,
in the Crimson Red
and bring the color
out to opposite sides
of the paper.

My brush now goes in
the jar of water
and I get up to make
a cup of tea,
letting the paint settle and dry
before continuing
with another color

What will be next?
I have no idea, until
I sit back down again.

Blessings of Watercolor 2

Adding Cobalt Blue
to the Crimson Red
not sure what comes next.
That's what I love
about abstract.
It just is.

Letting my painting
rest again
for another day
and seeing what I want
to do next,
might add black,
pink, orange, yellow.

I have not seen
a sunset in a while,
might have to
create one myself.

Blessings of Watercolor 3

The beauty of watercolor,
the playfulness of the colors
and the way they flow.
Water can be used a little
or a lot to get the effect you want.

The colors blend and swirl,
hugging softly.
The colors should flow easily
from your brush,
sometimes making up its own mind
where it wants to lay down and rest.

Of course, watercolor will not
always play if you are working
towards a specific outcome

Today I added yellow and black
to my abstract,
not finished yet,
not my decision,
the painting will tell me when it is completed.

Blessings of Watercolor 4

Adding tendrils of life
to my painting,
stems in Hooker's Green,
leaves of Sap Green.

Painting coming to life.
Even abstract has life.
Something I'm just learning.

Tubes of colors are laid out
before me.
You'd think it would be
hard to choose,
but it is not.
My instincts kick in
and I reach for the color
that I know is next.

And the brush,
Which size?
That is often more difficult.
Start out with one size brush,
then choose another.
Until the sun breaks through
the clouds and makes me smile.

Spring Prayer

Crocuses peeking out
from cold, hard ground.
Refusing to be deterred
by Mother Nature's
fickle and indecisive ways.

Although Mother Nature
is fighting a battle
that is unanticipated,
all that she combats
is to keep herself and us
as things should be.

Quite a task Mother Nature has
fighting destruction, pollution,
pesticides and genocide
of all her creatures.

Sacredness and consciousness
are the things that will save her.
Wrapped in love and compassion.
Prayers lifted in Holy awareness
of every breathing thing.

A Polish Supper

Polish ancestry
strong in my blood.
Try to understand,
to comprehend
all that went on
in another country,
another war
that began and ended
before my birth.
Miłosz and Szymborska,
they must both be
present at my dinner.
Served simply, a simple fare,
for two humble people.
I would ask them
about poems I have read
and re-read, underlined
and dog-eared, pages 216 and 51.
I need to understand
how poetry kept them alive.

HAPPY EARTH DAY!

Although how happy is the Earth and the creatures that inhabit her?
Thoughtless destruction of rainforests so that cattle can graze for fast
food companies' profit and palm oil can be leached to produce
products that cannot be recognized by nature.
Let us not forget our precious resource, water, that we have abused to
the point of gagging filth all its ways, oceans, rivers, lakes and
streams.
The thought of killing for sport and profit to the point of extinction,
elephants, rhinos, gorillas, and chimps... the list is endless, but they
are not.
And can I bear to talk about those precious creatures that pollinate
for human benefit, the honeybees that cannot do what they were
designed to do without getting poisoned by man who thinks he can
outsmart nature?
I ask you, can the Earth be saved? Can we?

"For this says the Lord,
The creator of the heavens,
Who is God,
The designer and maker of the earth
Who established it.
Not creating it to be a waste
But designing it to be lived in..."
—Isaiah 45:18

Autumn Song

The smell of cider in the crisp air,
the songs of geese heading south.
My desire to go with them,
the gift of picking up and leaving,
instincts leading the way.

But to follow them would mean
no more smells of apples
or sounds of dried leaves
crunching under foot,
the gift of the colors…

My eyes would miss
the gold, red, yellow, orange and brown.
The crisp, tart taste of apple cider
straight from the mill would no longer
be there to tempt my tongue.

After hiking through wooded land
I sit on a stump, left from a fallen tree.
Too old to no longer stand.
Looking around, knowing this is
right where I belong.

Sophia

Ancient Hymns
Ancient Temples
still ring with praise
to the Goddess Sophia.
She rises each morning
as the sun kisses the earth.
She cradles us with her radiance,
as the moon rises in soft slumber

Sophia, Goddess of Wisdom,
so willing to share
a gift too many find useless
amidst concrete and steel.

Brain power, manpower,
cloud the skies, and minds,
so we can no longer see her beauty,
or feel her Grace, much less
be silent enough to hear her Wisdom.

Can I know you,
oh great Goddess of Wisdom
who both rides the wind
and yet is the wind itself?

"She is more beautiful than the sun and excels every
Constellation of the stars"
—Wisdom 7:29

The Abyss

Hold me close
as the air chills.
If only in my dreams
you'd reach out to me,
if you can,
as blue skies
turn slate gray.
The emptiness in my heart
fills with tears
as the abyss grows wide
between us.

Sight Unseen

There are worlds unseen.
The cosmos, the stars,
the galaxies.

Here we have our morning routines,
our anger, our justified opinions
that overwhelm us.

And at the same time keep us safe
so that we don't think about what lies
beyond our meager lives that we
have created for safekeeping—

As if we were the ones in charge
of our own lives and this world
is truly run by angelic realms.

Sight Unseen.

Shifting with the Seasons

Feeling the subtle shift
in my cells as the leaves
do the same.

It's the same thing,
actually…

If you sit quietly
with the trees
you can feel the change;
the adjustment in nature
is ours as well.

That beauty you see
around you as the leaves change
is the same beauty that takes
place in your very self.

The beauty is there,
all around you,
and inside you
ready to burst forth
in stunning colors
that are seen in your smile,
felt in your hugs.

They are the gifts you bring
to this world.

To Know Is to Breathe

To take a deep breath
is to trust that there
will be another.
That trust which
is so often taken
for granted,
will rear its ugly head
when your lungs are restricted.
You are drowning
in the true sense
of the word.
Head under water
for too long a time.
But there are other ways…
when you have plunged
into love headfirst
only to find no one there,
no one to save you
from your own silly idea
of what love should be.
So you drown in despair,
your breath coming in
short gasps as the pain
of reality settles in.
Your lungs restrict when
the tears come too fast
and you try to hide
them in shame—
To trust in the next breath
is to trust life, your own,
no matter how it looks.

Breathe through the pain
Breathe through the fear
Breathe through the darkness
into the Light
of a new day.

The Chosen Few

It's cold,
in my heart, my bones
this night.

The world is ugly.
I no longer seek
to be part
of all that is going on.

This dark night
finds too many people
hungry for
a kind word—

But find none.

Too many,
like me,
hide in the warmth
of their homes.

It is only the forced
air heat
that keeps us warm.
Heat bought and paid for

By the souls out on the street.
The huddled masses
with no way to reach

The chosen few…

April

Renewal
precious Life,
shades of Pink
and Lavender dance
from the brown earth.

Fruit trees burst with color
and glorious scent.
Even the Song of Solomon
sings of the blossoming vines
after winter has passed.

Bunnies, foals, piglets, and calves
are born from the womb.
Chicks, ducklings, and goslings
break free from their shells.
You can hear their happy peeps.

Jesus opens the tomb
after three long days in darkness
to bring Light and Warmth
Peace and Love renewed
for all the Earth to sing
Hallelujah! Amen.

Ends

The end of life,
joy of a life well lived.
Sorrow for one that was not.

The end of a meal
followed by great conversation.
Or dishes done in silence.

The end of days,
Evening sunset brings
sorrow or peace

The end of creation,
the final act
of destruction

The end of the road,
dead end,

Decisions to be made.

The end of a love affair
pain, relief,
tears, sorrow.

Ends can sometimes be
what we make them.

Lost Keys and Rusted Chains

I see my future in the distance.
I see my past there too,
standing guard at the gate of my dreams.
The gate has been locked for so long,
the key having fallen out of
a hole in my pocket long ago.
There was a time of unconcern,
that left me with nothing.
Now only rusted chains hold my Spirit.
I see it all behind the gate.
The key wasn't all I lost from my pocket.
My soul holds a longing gaze for my heart.

Looking on the Bright Side

Shopping for a trip I have never taken.
The perfect outfit I will wear for eternity.
My time is short, but I am making the best of it.
I can put this designer gown on a credit card;
I will not have to worry about paying it off.

Do I wear it once on a whim for the hell of it?
What if I save the dress only to find out afterwards
that it is too late and it looks awful on me?
Better to try it on first, just to be sure.
What the hell—

Wear it to a bar that stays open after hours,
dance all night and drink more than I ever
have before, as well as putting a few rounds
for the rest of the patrons on my credit card
to make sure that it is maxed out.

Get that designer gown soaked and dirty
and give them all something to talk about
when they show up for my final act,
still smiling.

The Mercy of Silence

How much it is treasured but not sought out.
Currently where noise
has become the norm of the universe.
Boomboxes, earbuds, the louder the better,
Internet, satellite television, ringtones,
Twitter, Facebook, your duck lips out there,
expectancy of response, the oftentimes
very loud response of anger,
gunshots, sirens, cries in the night—
Turn it up, turn up those distractions
that keep you from hearing
the sorrows that tear at your heart…
Yes, drown it out, leave it to someone else.
It gets to be too much to bear.

Really, it's understandable
to just want to enjoy life
and not worry about the horror
that goes on in the world.

Until it hits home, and you are forced
to take out the earbuds,
turn down the noise
and face the music of reality.
Right in your own backyard.

A Holy Gift

Finding it so much easier to spend time
with the spiritual side of life found in nature.
I noted the slant in how I perceived the world,
as opposed to how the world expected to be perceived.
To be told that what I saw as meaningful was foolishness,
and would get me nowhere regardless of what
I knew to be holy.
The pleasure to be found in the presence of God
in the trees, the soil that was teaming with life.
Finding myself unable to move as the lightning
and thunder surrounding me caused me to tremble,
not with fear but understanding.
While everyone else ran inside, quickly closing windows,
I would run out.
And just as the clouds broke loose, I would fall to my knees
while rivulets poured forth both from my eyes and the sky,
to heal, to cleanse, to bring forth newness both inside and out.

More Real Than This

The hum of traffic
slow moving time.
Dawn is far off,
or so it seems.
Now sirens
in the distance;
someone's heart
is breaking
or has stopped.
As I wait for dawn
to break—
Is that a cry I hear?
Someone's bitter scream?
Sleep, if it will come,
will take it all away,
take me to another world
that is more real than this.

Rain

I hear tires on the rain-soaked streets
and on my window as it pounds the glass.
Just when I think it will slow down,
it starts up again harder than before.
I hate being alone on nights like this.

The rain beats the world
and I just want to yell for it to stop.
What is it about the rain that causes
so much anxiety in me? When it's
unrelenting I can't help but think

Of the blows that came hard and fast
as I covered my head—
the yelling sounds like thunder,
and the lightning is what I would see
when a punch made contact
with my eye. Make the rain stop.
Is it rain or is it tears? Just make it stop.
Please…

Silence

To love yourself enough
to love others even more
is the tallest order
when living a well-lived life
while on this Earth.

It's too easy to be dragged
down by what the outside
world says about you.
You can't let that stop you
from hearing the loving voice
of your Soul.

Silence must become
your friend so that
you can hear that tender voice
above all else.
The silence will bring you peace,
and make you whole.

Take Me Back...

Take me back
to where clear waters run
and dragonflies flit
with no fear

Take me back
to a time
when honeybees were healthy,
eagerly awaiting
the first blooms of spring

Take me back
to when elephants roamed
the great lands—where their tusks
and babies were safe to grow
to full strength

Take me back
to pure Love and a state
of Grace

Take me back
to smiles and laughter
that are known to all.

Take me back, just take me back.
Dear Mother of the Earth,
Mother of all...

The Sky Is Falling

Yes, Chicken Little, the sky is falling

in the form of rain and tears and bombs,

bringing with them grief and sorrow.

Praying for the sun to shine,

but the clouds keep coming.

Chicken Little what can we do

not to be destroyed by the fox

that is waiting… so sly, so vicious,

so cunning…

Do we have the courage to run the other way?

Not knowing what awaits…

Healing

The mind blows wide open with heat and freezing cold.
There are thoughts that terrify, but I keep focusing on them,
knowing that once they have broken,
scattered and returned to "normal," they will be laid out,
to see all that was hidden for protection from torment.

Something has caused this torrent, this ocean of feelings, but what?
Turning into a deluge that rides down the mountainous plains,
of cheeks and breasts.

The salt water that flows, first gathering at the abyss,
then like a surge, the waves pour out of the broken dam;
the body and mind that for so long
kept all things safe, all things hidden, have shattered
never to be put back the same way again.

The light comes shining to places that have been dark
with shame and self-hatred for too many years of desolation.
It hurts and feels good at the same time.
Does that make sense?

What has caused this pain to soften, to make room
for a new way of looking at the body with its scars
that no longer look ugly, but lovely? They show my strength,
they have served me well. I touch them for the first time with
tenderness,
smiling through tears.

So, what has burst this wall of protection? Ah! It is LOVE.

The Silence and the Struggle

There is no shortage of violence
in our streets and in our world.
We seek the silence of peace
in our hearts that too, eludes us.
Our breath becomes restricted.

And harsh with words
and thoughts of anger
that we did not know we were capable of—
The more we seek to stuff down
our ugliness, the more it rises up
and hurts us as much as it hurts others.

To forgive
To love
Too often these seem like insurmountable tasks
that leave us exhausted before we even begin.

Seemed like a good idea at the time
is a familiar refrain in our heads.
The famous saying, "The road to hell is…"
Yes, you know the one—in itself gives us

Comfort because of its truth,
the perfect scapegoat. We laugh and
we go on and the violence in our streets
and in our world continues.

Searching for peace that is just out of reach…

Gossip

Garbage that spews from mouths,
from lips wearing a hint of pleasure
that knows full well the destruction
that will follow in its wake.

The nasty smelly lies of half truths
that leave their home of sewage
to run down streets
knocking on doors, phones ringing
or pinging a text.

It can be one word, two or more,
it does not matter.
It always finds its mark.
Another mouth that loves
the taste of rotten garbage,

Destroyed lives.
And without a thought, the garbage
once again makes its way down the street
until the whole world stinks
to high heaven.

Coming from a mouth covering up
its own self-hate
with the satisfaction of making
someone else feel worse.

Precious Moments

Precious moments
tick by too quickly,
a second of eye contact
forgotten,
a hand held too briefly
but the warmth remains.
A hug,
a hug can occur,
with no message exchanged.

But then there are those hugs
between lovers
that can spark fires.
During those moments
when eye contact again
is made, and lingers, it becomes,
a gaze that becomes,
a smile, that becomes,
a kiss…

Precious moments
that are cherished
will last.

Leaving the Blame Behind

Turning the key in the lock
to open the door to the future,
or the past.

Trying to change things
for the better
but it seems whenever

I think I'm going forward
I realize I'm right back
where I started.

How does that happen?

I have always heard,
history repeats itself,
but I do not want it to.

It is like I am dragging
the chains of the past behind me
like Marley's ghost

Visions of changes I can
almost taste, like
the sweetest candy.

But I am always left with
sour grapes, the love
that I was sure was mine

What happened?

What did I do wrong this time?
Maybe it was not me.
I always blame myself.
Maybe I should leave the blame
in the past too.

Choose Life

The bitter cold
rests like a glacier
inside my heart.
It settled there,
some time ago

And has made itself
quite comfortable.
I can feel it.
Relaxed against my ribs
like it owns the place.

The bitter cold
does not care
if it takes
the breath from my lungs.
It knows only its own comfort,
that feeds on my loneliness,
and the sadness that envelops
my entire being.

It did not just come on its own,
I welcomed it with every
sad song that entered my ears
and every sad thought I chose
to dwell on.

The gift of choice is
the most beautiful gift
because it allows the sun to melt
the bitter cold in my heart.
It allows me to choose life
if I so choose.

A Holy Place Is a Living Book

To see inside the Sacred
is the gift of an open Soul.
A Soul that seeks and hungers
for the Divine.

To wait in silence
and anticipation,
for glorious Blessings
to come to the patient.

The blessed waiting
can take place anywhere.
A field, meadow, or cell,
the tenderness of the Divine
reaches all hearts who wait.

The book I mentioned
can be a tangible form,
or our hearts that open
at the becoming of God.

The whisper of Sophia
to wake us from our slumber,
our mundane way of living
to seek, to know, to believe.

Grace

Not just when the moon wanes,
should we shed what does not belong.
But every evening as the sun goes down,
we need to do the same;
continuing to grasp for that which has dried to dust,
only makes our souls wither.
Eyes that only look down and see
what has long been gone that will never see
the sun or the new growth that springs
from the Earth. Never allow the healing touch
that only the sun can provide to the Earth, to our Souls.
Look up, lift your hands, and be healed.
We may never learn why things come
into our lives and why they cannot stay,
but to try to hang on is destructive in every way.
When our hands are raised, they can be filled

With new things, beautiful things, joyful things.
How long will they stay, who can say?
Every moment is grace. Do not waste it.
Once you understand that everything changes,
including yourself, you can learn to stay
right here in this present moment and smile.

Did you know that it's your smile that causes
the sun to shine?

Stop 1

To stop in thought
In meditation
In prayer

To stop and behold
the beauty of it all,
the awareness
of our own bodies

To stop and wonder
how intricately
our bodies work,
each part in perfect harmony

To stop and smile
when you become aware
of the power and glory of it all.

Stop 2

To stop and see,
to really see
a bird in flight

To stop and stand
as the rain begins,
daring to let it
hit your upturned smile.

To stop and be touched
by the sight
of a perfect rose
that begs to be worshiped.

To stop and see
the beauty of the
Earth all around.

Words

Words are such gifts.
To write, to read,
to absorb through my skin
my eyes, my mind, my soul,
through every fiber of my being.
Words are magical,
taking me places
I have never been.
Yet through words,
I am able to taste foods
I've never eaten,
feel emotions that make me
catch my breath.
Words can stay with me
long after I have heard them,
or read them or written them down.
Letters that come together to form images,
so real and at times so frightening
that I can only sit for long periods of time
in the dark, absorbing the world
I have just entered and left.
Writing those words that flow
from my spirit, to pen, to paper,
I sit astonished and humbled to be
the vessel of something so powerful.

Faith

Some say it's easy
to have faith
to believe,
but for others,
it's so hard or impossible.
Those that think too much,
those that must see proof,
for them, faith is harder
to muster.
Faith comes from searching
the heart and the soul,
not the mind,
although searching
in books, universities, or asking scholars
may be a means to an end.
It has nothing to do with faith.
Faith is of Spirit and the Spirit
can be elusive to those trying
to find it in concrete ways.
Faith is found in silence,
where the Spirit dwells—the silence of the Heart.

Go search there.

Fickle Mother Nature

Tulips, daffodils,
still hiding
under frozen ground.

A few crocuses
have peeked their flowery
heads above ground.
Will they see the snow
headed our way?

They should have known
not to listen to the calendar.
It lies, lies all the time.
Yes, it says spring is here.

Yes, it is April,
Yes, Easter has passed.
But Mother Nature
makes up her own mind
when spring will arrive.

Just Be

Be the Wind.
Fierce and Forceful
Gentle and Delicate

Be the Water.
Strong and Powerful
Calm and majestic

Be the Earth.
Steadfast and Mighty
Beautiful and Plentiful

Be the Fire.
Uncontrolled in Rage
Dancing in Freedom

Be the Spirit.
Love Itself
Healing in Joy

Be the One.
Who is all of this—
Wind, Water, Earth, Fire, Spirit

Fierce
Strong
Steadfast
Uncontrolled
Love

But also

Gentle
Calm
Beautiful
Dancing
Healing

Be the One who is all of this and more.

The Power of Words

There is a lot of power
in words,
in writing,
in believing in my words,
my feelings,
my life.

There is always a catch,
"Ah, but what if…,"
Fuck the 'what if.'
Nothing is proven,
until it is accomplished.

You can assume all you want,
or let someone else assume for you,
(There are plenty around who like to do that)
or you can trust your life
to carry you to better things.

To step out of an assumption
into reality is brave and powerful.
Do it more often.
You will find you are not broken.
You are free.

Leaves of My Life

Watching the golden leaves fall
so easily and willingly

They let go, taking off, like birds,
trusting the current of the wind
to take them softly to the ground

Unlike myself when surrender is needed,
fighting and resisting,
fearful and anxious

Oh Lord, may I learn to be trusting
like the leaves.

Letting go, falling, knowing
your Spirit will hold me up
until I land safely in Your arms.

Seeking Clear Skies

I hear the wind picking up outside my window.
The rain is sure to follow,
along with gloomy days
that fit my dark moods,
that cling like the drops of rain on my window.

I seek clear skies and bright days
that lift me from the darkness
that surrounds my heart.

Patience, trust, and faith
are all words I know
but have not diligently practiced.

The continuous days of darkness and gloom
bring me down to where patience, trust, and faith,
do not dwell.
I must learn to seek higher realms
where angels of light wait with celestial greetings
to heal my wounded soul.

Whisper

The whisper
of God's voice
can be heard above
a thunderclap,
city traffic,
the screams
in your own head.

The habit
of just being still
can bring this about.

God's still small voice
like your lover's whisper
as he nuzzles your neck,
brings you chills and goosebumps.

Love will do that.
God's love is everywhere.
And to hear His voice
all we need to do
is still and listen.

Making Love from Yarn

To create with needles and yarn
something that is made
to bring comfort, to bring smiles.
To bring a sense of safety
for those who wear, curl up in,
or even play with—

Cat toys with catnip hidden inside.
Blankets for stray dogs
that have found shelter.
Chemo caps for those fighting cancer.
Prayer shawls for widows feeling lonely.
Hats, scarves, and mittens for the homeless
or for children of struggling families

Afghans, baby blankets and sweaters
to show love—
The list is endless—never ending.
When you have found your gift,
use it to bring comfort,
to bring a smile.

Snow

Snow is softly falling.
On this April morning,
spring will come in its time,
when snow is spent
and gives way to rain.

To trust and believe
in the changing
of the seasons

But for now,
snow continues
to fall.

Believe in its beauty.
While it is with us
soon heat
will be upon us
and we will wish
for the kiss of snow.

Writing

What is it about writing,
putting pen to paper
that opens my soul?
It is not the ink
from the pen that writes my words.
It is the blood from my veins,
and the salt of tears and sweat
from my wounds
that create what pours out.

My pen doesn't stop
until I am empty for the day,
and I lay spent, exhausted
or sometimes refreshed,
so grateful for the time I spend,
pen in hand, pouring my heart
upon the page.

Birds

3 am
Very loud chirping
is heard.
It is still dark,
but somehow
the birds know
that another day has begun,
and they are happy!

I wish someday,
to open my eyes
at 3 am to sing,
but I am afraid
I'm more like the crow
with its raspy caw! caw!,
telling the rest of the
birds to go back to sleep.

Deep in Your Spirit

Deep in your Spirit
lies a wellspring of Joy.
We get to it by digging deep.
The tool we use is Faith.

Faith we use for what cannot be seen,
but what we know and believe
to be true.
Faith is a shovel with a pointed end
that can penetrate, with enough
determination, all the barriers
that block our way to Joy.

Is it easy?
Too often not.
It takes sweat, grit and tears.
Is it worth it?
Always.

The Buddhist saying
"No Mud, No Lotus"
is true.
You must be willing to clear out
the debris to get to where
the beautiful lotus of Joy lies waiting.
It comes with laughter and Peace.
So, dig. Dig deep
for your treasure of Joy.

Webs

Life can become a web
if we let it.
It can be our own design
that we create to keep others out
and make us feel safe.
Or it can be a web
that we allow others to create for us
because we do not trust ourselves
to make our own.

Webs can be an illusion,
a beautiful design that keeps us
entranced so we don't look
any further.
It can be complicated in design,
or simple,
one that takes days to create,
or just hours.
It doesn't really matter.
We are still stuck.

This World Today

The wind is whirling.
Things are scrambled.
Fear is a real thing,
and no longer the creation
of one's imagination.
Smoke comes up to cloud
what needs to be seen.
The starving
The diseased
The unloved

The earth belching
sewage and pain.
There is a rush
by the ghosts with bulging eyes
grasping at everything.

And those that weep
while tenderly trying
to save life in all
its forms.

May those who weep
win this battle,
strong in their
Tenderness and Love.

The Wind

It can blow so gently
against face and hair,
making you smile.
Gentle wind on a
warm sunny day
is perfection
to those who notice
and are grateful.

If you cannot notice
the gentle wind,
Mother Nature can
also send strong winds
to knock out power lines,
knock over cars, trees,
and destroy houses.
Now that will get
your attention.

Maybe if you notice
the gentle breeze
that kisses your cheek

In gratitude, more often
Mother Nature will not
have to send the stronger wind
to get your attention.

The Wind 2

The wind
is whipping
whipping
whipping
as I go
slipping
slipping
slipping
down the recesses
of my mind

My thoughts cannot
seem to settle.
Tossing and turning,
my intuition is on alert,
but I'm not sure
for what or why.
It is like trying to
tame a cyclone.

All I can do is try
to sleep, in hopes

That my dreams will
give me answers
to questions I do not know
I have.

Stillness

A breeze is blowing,
and autumn leaves
are falling to the ground
like colorful snowflakes

A fleeting season
that shows us the best
Nature has to offer.
You're wise if you stop to witness it.

All the shades of brown,
yellow, red, and orange.
Some trees look like they are ablaze
when the sun hits them.

Taking your breath away
until the clouds come
to obscure the sun
and the magic is gone.

Autumn teaches us
that we can be taught
to stop and focus on
what is right in front of us.

The wind blows away
the beauty so fast we cannot waste
a second anywhere but right here
in this very moment.

Changing of Seasons

So, autumn has begun,
but the dog days of summer
are dragging on,
giving us one last touch
of what we are leaving behind.
Those tired of summer heat, groan,
enough already, they say.
But sure as the cold winds blow,
they will whip us inside,
to make hearty soups and stews,
bringing out yarn of wool and needles
to make sweaters for loved ones,
and those less fortunate.

Hold each day dear to your heart,
for it is gone too soon, like loved ones,
like leaves with their days spent
turning golden, then brown, then feeding
the Earth for another round come spring.

After months of frozen earth and dormancy,
always know that there is a change coming,
and it will bring its own beauty.
Yes, patience is a virtue.

Seeing Through Smoke and Ash

I shut my eyes tight,
but I still see the images,
of fires and smoke
of death and terror.
Those who are so bravely
fighting the fires
that surround them.
Those who flee in terror.
Those who try to flee,
only to be taken over
by the overwhelming flames

Crying out to God to save
all that they have worked for.
Above all, their very lives
and the thousands of lives
of the innocents,
the creatures that call
these areas home.
Their Spirits rise to heaven

Carried by the smoke,
while their ashes fall
back to Earth like snowflakes

Many see the ash not realizing
these are the very ashes of the dead.

Honor these ashes—
Take a handful, place them
on your altar.
Pray for them, as you would
the ashes of your ancestors.

Silent Screams

Everyone in their own way
screaming to be heard
in the silence of the
very loud written word
or creative art.

What were the thoughts
or feelings of cavemen/women
who first carved or drew
pictures on cave walls?
A desire to be seen or understood.

Those who frequent city streets
with spray cans to create
gang signs and art
on abandoned buildings.
Wanting to be seen,
wanting to be heard.

The high school girl feeling
lonely, insecure, unloved
writes behind closed doors
on bathroom stalls,
wanting her feelings to be validated.

How old were you when you knew
you had to find a way
to let out all that was inside
before it ate you alive?

Was it a form of art
or written word?

Let it out any way you can.

You need to for your own salvation.
And if you see graffiti on buildings,
words or art carved into bathroom stalls,
listen, listen for the silent scream.

You just might save a life.

Acknowledgment

A few of my poems from this collection were previously published, for which I would like to express my deep gratitude.

"For the Bees." *Journey of the Heart: An Anthology of Spiritual Poetry by Women* (2014). Edited by Catherine Ghosh.

"A Trusting Heart" and "Grace." *Where Journeys Meet: The Voice of Women's Poetry* (2015). Edited by Catherine Ghosh & The Journey of the Heart Poets.

"Dreams and Other Fairy Tales." *Poetry as a Spiritual Practice* (2016). Edited by Catherine Ghosh, with Sandra Marie Allagapen, Jamie Burgess, Jesse James, and Tammy T. Stone.

"Sophia." *Goddess: When She Rules* (2017). Edited by Catherine L. Schweig, with Sandra M. Allagapen, Julia W. Prentice, and Tammy Stone Takahashi.

www.ingramcontent.com/pod-product-compliance
Lightning Source LLC
Chambersburg PA
CBHW031218270326
41931CB00006B/608